HOW TO BE A
HAPPY SINGLE MOTHER

An Inspirational Guide to Parenting Alone

ORIT SUTTON

Eloquent Books
New York, New York

Eloquent Books

An imprint of AEG Publishing Group

845 Third Avenue, 6th Floor - 6016

New York, NY 10022

www.eloquentbooks.com

ISBN 978-1-60860-730-3

Printed in the United States of America

To Sophia,
for the sheer happiness and pure love.

CONTENTS

ACKNOWLEDGMENTS

I must start by thanking my family: your staggering support has been totally invaluable. I am enveloped by your warmth, generosities of every kind and immense love, and I shall never forget how you are always there for me. It is said that 'you can't choose your family' — but I wouldn't choose any other even if I could; I'm a very lucky lass and I love you all so very much.

I must also profusely thank my dear friends: knowing you believe in me and love me is always such a comfort and source of energy.

I'd also like to thank Avril and all of my other colleagues: your vision, support, energies and, above all, trust in me, enables me to work with creativity and passion. Work is a pleasure, as are your friendships.

Many thanks to my publishers for giving me the opportunity to share my experiences and thoughts with others in similar situations, and for potentially giving me a whole new parallel career!

Thank you to anyone who ever smiles at me in a shop, lets me into the traffic, is helpful on the phone or is polite and friendly in any way: you ease me through my day and lift my spirits.

And, of course, my deepest gratitude goes to my *raison d'etre* — Sophia.

Thank you.

INTRODUCTION

Relatively few people plan on being a single parent — and I'm pretty sure no one actually dreams of it as they grow up. But a huge number of women and more and more men find themselves living with, and often raising their child or children, alone.

At eight months pregnant, and then again when my daughter was four months old (with an attempt at reconciliation with my husband in between), I became a single mum. And so the dream was over — living with the man I loved and our child was not to be. I have had to shift my expectations: re-draw my hopes and beliefs about what makes me happy, what's important and how I want to raise my child. Fundamentally, I have had to rediscover who I am. But, within these apparently devastating circumstances, I have found a surprisingly wonderful life in which my daughter and I can be extremely happy.

If you are shocked, humiliated, terrified, furious, overwhelmed, utterly exhausted and, by turns, numb and in more emotional pain than you thought possible, I know what you're going through — I've been there.

I would like to share my experiences and discoveries with you. Your situation might seem bleak and desperate, but let me hold your hand. However painful things are now, I can help you turn your life around with positive thinking, practical ideas and a lot of love.

I've written and structured this book with you, an exhausted and time-poor single mother, in mind. If you are too tired and too busy to read it through, dip into it: just read a section or two when you feel the need of a little company, support, guidance or inspiration. You can also contact me for help and advice (see my contact details at the end of the book): you needn't be alone.

At the point of finishing this book, my daughter is just over two-and-a–half years old. I have, therefore, used the feminine pronoun when referring to a child, and based a lot of my writing on life with a toddler. But this book is for all single mothers with one or many children, of either gender and of any age.

This book is for you.

THE SINGLE MOTHER'S MANIFESTO

Sure, we are restricted with the hours we can work, the money we can earn, the people we can see, and the places we can go, but we are not restricted with the laughter we can share and the love we can give and receive: no one can restrict our minds or our hearts.

Let's redefine single-parent families and the people within them. No longer shall we be the scapegoats for societal ills, producing troublesome children and sponging off the state. We shall not be ashamed or embarrassed, and shall use the term 'Single Mother' with pride. We are complete, united and loving families, within which both adults and children can thrive and flourish. We produce stable, functional, happy people who communicate, contribute and lead: people who hold down good jobs and have healthy, rewarding relationships. We value ourselves and others. We are not second-class citizens: we choose freedom, success, health and happiness.

PLUSES OF SINGLE PARENTING

◆ You don't have to deal with anyone's crap.

◆ You can make the decisions in your own home.

◆ You can form an incredibly close bond with your child.

◆ If your ex-partner takes your child for a night/ weekend, you can get a real break that many parents with partners at home don't get.

◆ You are free to 'be'.

GETTING IT ALL DONE AND COPING

DON'T MULTI-TASK!

Not the important stuff anyway! Yes, I know, women are meant to be brilliant at multi-tasking and despair at men when they can't, but men just might be onto something. It's fine to do a mindless chore, like folding clean washing while your child is engrossed in colouring a picture, and you can still interact with her when she wants to. But, don't try to write an important email that requires all of your concentration just when your help is needed on a complicated piece of maths homework.

DEMARCATE TIME

Set aside as much 'sacred' time with your child as possible: time just for the two of you and, ideally, with no interruptions. Plan your day carefully so that you can 'wear your different hats' separately and concentrate on each job properly. This is especially important if you work at home: don't attempt to mother, work and cook all at the same time — you'll end up with a neglected child, a missed deadline, burnt pasta and a very frazzled you!

BE SUPER-ORGANISED!

- Devise a routine that works for you so you know what you're doing and when.

- Keep on top of the mess so that you don't waste time and effort finding things.

- Diarise sending birthday and anniversary cards a week before they are due.

- Don't make one long 'To Do' list. If you know you'll be near the shops on Friday, write everything you need to buy on Friday's page in your diary.

- Plan quick meals for the days you'll be home late and cook properly on more relaxed days, involving your child if possible. You can also cook double quantities and freeze half to be used on the rushed evenings.

- Think ahead: if your child is going to a party on Saturday afternoon, diarise buying and wrapping a present on a day when you'll have the time and opportunity, and even plan what she's going to wear — and make sure it's clean!

- Keep on top of returning calls and emails, thanking people when necessary and filing paperwork.

◆   Make sure all your bills are paid by Direct Debit or
    Standing Order so you don't need to think about them
    every month.

◆   Put out bags/clothes/anything needed for the next day the
    evening before.

THROW OUT OR STORE

Once a week, I potter about the house and have a good sort
out. Any bits and pieces I haven't kept on top of I file away,
recycle, bag-up for charity or, as a last resort, throw out. I bag up
old bread for a trip to the duck pond, put a couple of old-ish toys
in a store box, display any paintings my daughter has done, check
'use by' dates on food in the fridge and generally shape
everything up. As I de-clutter my home it de-clutters my mind…
it's wonderfully cathartic!

ACCEPT HELP

My mum and her partner are brilliant with helping me out.
They look after my daughter once a week and are always happy
to pop to a shop for me or collect something in their area. I know
they and my daughter adore these days together, and the errand-
running saves me so much time and effort. Don't be too proud to
accept help if you are lucky enough to be offered it — it can make
a huge difference to your life, and favours can always be
returned.

NOT GETTING IT DONE

Sometimes, you just have to accept that you simply can't do it all: you are only one person and nobody is superhuman.

I hate it when things don't go according to plan. When I was trying to finish writing this book, a number of setbacks made me so frustrated I was close to tears. At one point, my daughter got an ear infection and I just had to re-order my priorities: she needed me and the work would have to wait. The most important thing was to make her comfortable and secure while she recuperated, and then be enormously thankful when she was well again.

SURVIVING SLEEP DEPRIVATION

This is the biggie — the killer. A chronic shortage of sleep is so debilitating it makes even simple tasks seem like mountains and, over a period of time, can lead to physical and mental illness. I have much sympathy for anyone suffering from baby-related sleep deprivation. For the first few months of my daughter's life, she fed every two hours — sometimes even more frequently. I was so exhausted that I hallucinated, speaking coherently was a struggle, and I became used to my head spinning with the slightest movement. But, there are ways of easing this agony and making life a little more bearable.

EAT YOUR WAY TO ENERGY

When you're dog-tired and surrounded by dirty pots, the last thing you feel like doing is cooking healthy, balanced meals. But, this is ESSENTIAL if you are to have the energy and resilience you'll need for bringing up a child. It's tempting, of course, to reach for a quick caffeine or chocolate fix when you're desperately tired and have a million things to do, but these stimulants will give you a sudden surge of energy followed by a slump. Similarly, eating takeaways and ready meals, with their high levels of fat and salt, might give you the immediate comfort and convenience you crave, but this will be short-lived and you'll soon crash again.

Slow energy releasers which keep your blood sugar levels steady, such as porridge, pasta and wholemeal bread, will improve your mood, alleviate a little of the fatigue, and make you feel a whole lot better in the long-run. When I hit a wall, dried fruit gives me a real boost. Also, try to eat loads of fresh fruit and veg — it really will make a big difference to your general wellbeing.

DRINK PLENTY OF WATER

Enough said.

VITAL VITAMINS

Although gaining all your necessary minerals and vitamins through food is ideal, this is rarely possible when you're rushed and exhausted. Supplement your diet with a vitamin tablet suitable for your body at this time. If you're breastfeeding, be especially careful what you take: one designed for pregnant and breastfeeding women is best, and should always be checked out with your health care provider.

GET THE BALANCE

People used to say to me, "sleep when your baby sleeps". This is a ridiculous and highly annoying piece of advice! Had I followed such 'pearls of wisdom', the flat would have drowned in dirty clothes, there would never have been any hot meals or clean plates, and I wouldn't have showered for months! There are so many tasks to catch up on when your little one finally drops off that it's simply not possible to leave everything and climb into bed. However, some things really can wait. I'm dreadful at knowing when to stop and grab a little shut-eye, but there are times when sleep simply must be prioritised over everything else!

ACCEPT HELP

As mentioned in the previous chapter, don't be a martyr and try to do everything yourself. You have nothing to prove and everything to gain from letting those around you help out and make your life a little easier. Both you and your child will suffer if you become exhausted and ill and, when you are able, you can always return the favours.

Sleep oh blessed sleep,
the place where I can dream,
of all that I do need
my energy to keep.

Sleep oh blessed sleep,
The place of future hope,
in places far away,
and love for me to keep

Sleep oh blessed sleep
Lull me with your content,
Keep me ever safe my
soul's sanity to keep.

Sleep oh blessed sleep,
Let me emerge at morn,
With clearer thought and mind,
with no more need to weep

Susan Alldred Lugton

DADDY

Whether you like it or not, your child's father is a crucial person in your child's life and, by proxy, your life. If he wants to be an available and hands-on father, even though you are no longer together, your child will benefit enormously, and you should do everything you can to facilitate this. It can be tough — really tough — but dig deep and make it work.

YOUR BEHAVIOUR AND YOUR CHILD'S WELLBEING

I believe that the manner in which you and your ex communicate, treat each other, arrange access and generally conduct yourselves, can make or break your child. Whatever has happened in your relationship and however much pain and anger you feel, it is important to remember that you are both the adults. Your child needs to be protected from rows, bad atmospheres, negative emotions and disturbing situations at all costs; never ever make her a pawn or use her to manipulate or force your ex to yield to your wishes; never compete for your child's affections with gifts and treats. As an innocent child, she must be kept well out of any negotiations, emotional game-playing or point-scoring: the break-up of your adult relationship has absolutely nothing to do with her and it must stay that way. Don't EVER bad-mouth or criticise her father in front of your child: if you want to slag him off, call a friend.

Your child should NEVER feel torn between the two of you, guilty about spending time with one of you or be asked to keep secrets from one or other parent. This can seriously screw-up a child — DON'T DO IT!

COMMUNICATION

Talk REGULARLY and talk PRIVATELY with your ex. Don't let things build up until they erupt in front of your child. Call each other or talk face-to-face when your child is in bed or at school, and make sure that you are on the same page and both as happy as possible with current arrangements. Be flexible and open to change as your child grows up and circumstances change.

Privately talking with my ex has been vital in being able to relate to him amicably in front of our daughter. It has often been highly emotional, but we have both begun to slowly understand a little of the other's pain and realise some of the things that went wrong between us. One thing I have had to learn is patience: I am a person who likes things to be sorted out quickly and neatly, but this is just not possible where broken relationships are concerned.

Human emotions are messy, ever-changing and, of course, extremely personal. I have had to really listen. I have often had to reign-in my own pain and anger for the sake of progressing the conversation and not getting stuck in negative mud-slinging. And I have also had to allow the rebuilding of civil and amicable communication to be slow and take its own course.

PUT YOURSELF IN YOUR CHILD'S SHOES

Obviously, every situation is different. If a child is very young and has never lived with her father — or doesn't remember doing so, it is completely different from a father leaving the family home when a child is a young adolescent, for example. But, in all cases, altruism, empathy and strength are crucial in your own behaviour. At every step I always ask myself, 'how would this feel for my daughter? If I were her, would this situation be comfortable and make me happy, or not?' This is my failsafe guide, my bright star.

RESPECT YOUR EX

At first it was terribly painful. Anger, pain and resentment made it practically impossible for me to treat my daughter's father with any respect; I just didn't feel he deserved any. But then I realised that it wasn't about whether he deserved it or not, nor was it about my opinion of him or his behaviour — it was all about what would make our daughter a confident, emotionally-secure and very happy person. Witnessing her mum being so bitter and angry that she was unable to be civil to her dad was certainly not going to achieve this! Whenever I was tempted to make a snide remark or a bitter recrimination, I would look at my daughter and think, 'DO WHAT'S BEST FOR HER!'

Don't ever undermine your ex as a parent — and especially not in front of your child. If he says or does anything that you have an issue with, again, talk to him privately. Treat your ex with respect and dignity and you might be amazed at the way he steps up and starts really embracing his responsibilities — and he might treat you with some respect too! Give him a chance — he is undoubtedly hurting too. Lighten up a bit and ask yourself, 'What's the worse that can happen?' You've produced this amazing child together, now work together to make sure she is the healthiest, most successful and happiest she can be.

I am lucky that my ex also wants what is best for our daughter. He has worked very hard with me to achieve a calm and amicable atmosphere whenever he visits. I make sure he is welcome and comfortable in my home — our daughter's home — and he makes sure he is respectful in my space but also relaxed. He regularly looks after our daughter while I am working and we sometimes all go out together or kick about at home. It can be hard and a complete head-mess when we appear to be a happy family out in public, but I am caring less about this as time goes on. According to statistics, there are many families who do live together and are far less happy. We don't have to justify or explain our situation to anyone. Our daughter adores her father and he adores her.

CO-PARENTING: PARENTING TOGETHER WHEN APART

Just because you are not living together or in a relationship, and just because you do not conform to a societal norm, does not mean you cannot co-parent. Making important decisions together, in areas such as schooling and vaccinations, is hugely beneficial for everyone. If your ex is not a user of drugs or drink, and is generally being a good father, he deserves a say in your child's life. Involving him in some of your daily decisions can also help him in his parenting. He may not want to be with you, but this doesn't mean he does not want to be with his child, and he now has to cope with living away from her and can feel extremely impotent and frustrated. If he is involved in her routine he will certainly be a better dad.

REMEMBER: IF YOUR CHILD BENEFITS, DO IT!

PRESENTING A UNITED FRONT

All children — not only those living in a lone-parent family — try to play their parents off to their advantage. If your child is not living with her father and she knows that he may not always be aware exactly what she is or isn't allowed to do, it is especially important that you and he present a united front. Don't allow your child to come between you and your ex as parents. If she gets away with it regularly she could become extremely manipulative and deceitful, which will run through into other relationships she has in later life.

The above are all ideals, and none of it is easy to say the least. You will probably feel like telling your ex to f-off on regular occasions, and he will want to say the same back. Slamming the door on him and getting on with it on your own will often seem like the easiest and emotionally-safest option, but your child really will be a different and much happier person if both her mum and dad can cooperate and, who knows — go with me on this one and don't throw the book across the room! — maybe even be friendly or (*deep breath*) friends...?!

WORKING

Unless your ex is very wealthy and very generous (unlikely!), you will undoubtedly have to work. Indeed, you may actually want to work, whatever your financial situation. Working and raising a child can be exhausting and a logistical nightmare for any parent. If you are a lone parent, juggling it all can be extremely challenging. But, with some careful planning and a bit of luck, it can actually benefit everyone and have huge advantages.

HOURS AND AREA

The amount you work — or don't work — is critical to your child's wellbeing, especially when she is young. More and more employers now offer flexible working times, job shares and opportunities to work at home (see 'Useful Websites'). If you are in education, you will keep similar times to your child's schooling hours and have the extra benefit of the long holidays.

Being self-employed can offer the opportunity of working at home and finishing work in the evenings.

Every sort of employment can have its perks, and they will undoubtedly have their drawbacks too. Being answerable to a boss can be highly stressful if your child is ill and you just can't make it in, while working at home can mean that you are always surrounded by your work and can never switch off. If at all possible, try to do something that is as enjoyable and rewarding as possible (although I am well aware that this is not an option for everyone). If you are happy and satisfied with your work, you will have more positive energy for your child rather than being drained and frustrated.

More and more mums, motivated by having control over their own hours and being able to work from home, have set up their own internet businesses. There are franchise opportunities, job shares, and many other options out there. If you're not happy, look about, research the possibilities: you don't have to be stuck in a job which is making you miserable and keeping you away from your kids for long hours.

CHILDCARE

If you are very lucky, your ex, your own mum and other relatives will all be able to pitch-in and share looking after your child while you are working. Most mothers don't have such a wonderful situation, however, and need some professional childcare for at least part of every week; this needn't be a negative situation for you or your child if you spend time finding a childminder, nanny or nursery with whom your child is happy and who you trust implicitly.

All childcare providers in Britain must be Ofsted-registered and monitored, and you should check and read the reports carefully. Your best guide, however, is always your intuition: if you are at all uneasy about leaving your child with anyone, simply DON'T! Even if there is no real reason for this feeling, trust your gut. Similarly, your child's reactions will also be a good guide: if she is happy and eager to go in the morning, and chatty and relaxed when she returns, you know you are doing the right thing; if she is at all withdrawn or unhappy, find out what's going on and move her immediately!

GUILT

Even if you have a wonderful childminder or your mum provides loving and stimulating childcare full-time, there will be days when you just feel terribly guilty about leaving your child and working. I am often torn in two, missing my daughter while at work and trying not to think of all the work I have on while spending time with my child. This is natural and can't always be avoided. Try not to compensate by lavishing gifts on your child when you see her, or letting her play you and get everything she wants. Children can smell guilt a mile off and will use it to their advantage to gain treats, avoid bedtimes and generally run you ragged — even if they are perfectly happy when you are working.

When you return home, don't push your child to hug and kiss you if she is happy playing or needs a little time to warm up with you again. Young children especially can be very fickle, and will often feel closest to the person they have spent most time with that day, or will just be happy to know you are back. Just because you need reassurance that everything is okay, doesn't mean she does!

THE BENEFITS

Although this is a hugely controversial area, a report published by the University of Bristol's Centre for Market and Public Organisation in 2003 — and again in the February 2005 issue of the Economic Journal — showed evidence that children's cognitive development did not suffer if they were placed in good quality childcare as opposed to being with their mum full-time. In fact, the study showed that the children who were slower with speaking, and then reading and writing later on, were the ones who had been cared for by an unpaid friend or relative full-time from an early age. This suggests that child minders and nurseries can be highly stimulating and educational for children, and can balance the love and protection provided by a grandparent. The report also found that, in families where the mother worked, the child did not miss out on much parental contact because mum cut back on her own 'me' time and dad became more involved with childcare. I'm sure we can all identify with having very little time and space for ourselves, but the dad contact is also extremely important (see chapter 'Daddy').

If you get the childcare right and enjoy your work (and I know this can be a very tall order!), both you and your child can gain a great deal from time spent apart. Other people caring for your child can never be a substitute for you, and must only ever complement and enhance the love, attention and re-assurance you alone can provide. In the right environment, however, and with the right people, your child can develop as a confident, independent person away from your apron strings, and you can find the fulfilment and personal space you need for your own confidence and identity. You will also be providing an excellent role model of a modern, independent woman who doesn't need to choose between a family or career, but who can successfully combine the two and meet the demanding needs of a child or children — and herself. The time then spent with your child can be much more precious and rewarding, and you can really put it to good use and enjoy each other's company.

GOVERNMENT BENEFITS

In the short-term, benefits can be a real life-saver and help you get back on your feet. The Tax Credit system in the UK means that many people don't have to choose between employment and the dole: if you work the required number of hours per week and are still on a low income, you may be entitled to Government top-ups, which can be invaluable in helping you to pay some essential expenses, such as childcare. For information and to apply, check out the Tax Credits' website: http://www.hmrc.gov.uk/TAXCREDITS/.

I would not recommend relying on benefits for long though. For your own self-esteem, and as a good example to your child, aim to be financially independent as soon as it is realistically feasible.

GRAB OPPORTUNITIES

MAKE THEM HAPPEN.
YOU CAN DO IT — LOOK
AT WHAT YOU'VE ALREADY
DONE: STUFF YOU'D NEVER
HAVE DREAMED OF
GETTING THROUGH A FEW
YEARS AGO, I BET!

POSITIVE PARENTING

I have heard many women saying that they will 'give up' 5 years to stay at home and raise a couple of kids and then they will return to work. This makes it sound like a prison sentence! It is hard enough for mothers in a relationship, but combining work and raising a child when you're a single parent can seem almost impossible. But we don't need to shelve our dreams and our very identities when we give birth: you, mum, should always be the default, the rock, often in the foreground and ALWAYS there, even if only in your child's head and heart. If your child knows when she will see you and that you will be emotionally present and engaged when you are together, she will be much happier to spend time with other people when you need to work.

I am convinced that time spent with grandparents, other family members, childminders, other children and friends, is incredibly valuable and actually necessary for a child to really develop as a whole and confident person. Your child learns how to interact differently with a variety of people, and realises that she cannot always be the centre of attention. As long as she is with someone who loves, stimulates and protects her, you can relax.

Your child will also see that her mum has ambitions, dreams, goals, several demands on her time and her own needs. She will have a strong role model of a working, independent woman with an interesting and fulfilling life. The caveat to all this is, of course, that when you are together you shouldn't try to work at the same time. As I discussed in 'Getting it All Done', time with your child is sacred: don't try to finish that email, hang-up the washing, return a call and pay a bill. Instead, sit on the floor and really listen to your child, take her lead when she suggests games, make lots of eye contact, smile, encourage and chat away; organise trips out, visits to friends and family, and creative activities at home.

RESPECT AND DISCIPLINE

Treat your child with the respect and dignity with which all humans should treat each other; if you make a mistake, apologise; if something is new, confusing or different, explain; when your child is feeling adventurous and independent, give her freedom and space; when she is needy and vulnerable, give her extra love and support. If these conditions prevail, then you can also structure in boundaries and provide the discipline that all children need. Although you can be friends and have a two-way relationship, at the end of the day, you are the boss: you are older, wiser and know what is best for her. Bedtime is bedtime, and a firm 'no' means just that: don't let guilt about being a single parent or having to work — or anything else — mean that you allow rules to be broken, treats to be too regular and unappreciated, and discipline to break down.

AGE-APPROPRIATE RESPONSIBILITY

As a single parent, it can be easy to rely too heavily on your child for practical help and even emotional support; a little responsibility — like helping to tidy her bedroom once a day — is fine, but children need a childhood and must not have worries and burdens. Don't make her take on large and tiring household chores or regular childcare duties of younger children. She should never be made to feel guilty that you have too much work or you're exhausted or can't get a babysitter. Don't tell her that you are lonely or frustrated: if you are, talk to a friend. Allow her to have a childhood, full of play and innocence, and don't make her a substitute partner.

It can be easy to confuse an intelligent, bright child for an emotionally mature one. If your child readily comprehends and is very sharp, don't mistake this for being able to cope with emotional issues which are beyond her years. In fact, the more intelligent a child, the more sensitive they can often be as they are so aware and imaginative, and extra precautions should be taken to shield them from only the most age-appropriate conversations and situations.

EMOTIONAL SECURITY

Similarly, your child should feel that you are emotionally strong and capable. You are the adult and she is safe with you: she should not return from school to find you undressed and tear-stained. Don't take to your bed and force her to fend for herself when you are upset: if you are having a hard time, seek help from another adult — don't burden your child with worry way beyond her years.

THE ILLUSION OF CONTROL GOES A LONG WAY

Although it may often feel as if your child is calling the shots, young children especially should actually have very little, if any, control over their own lives: she is often told who she is seeing when, what to eat, when to sleep and what to wear. And so, giving your child just a little say in everyday decisions can really help alleviate her frustrations and prevent a constant battle of wills. Depending on your child's age, present her with an appropriate amount of freedom within a structure that she can handle.

A two-year-old, for example, will love the feeling of power when you ask if she wants to wear the pink dress or the blue trousers, but often won't be able to cope with a more open-ended question of 'What do you want to wear today?' Similarly, presenting two options at dinnertime, before anything is cooked, can avoid a lot of tantrums. But once a meal has been chosen and prepared, it has to be eaten, and your child shouldn't be allowed to suddenly refuse the presented dish and choose something different again.

More important issues, such as crossing the road safely and wearing a seat belt, should not be up for negotiation. If you are confused about what is considered to be the best practice, you should ideally talk it through with your ex if he is around. If not, chat with another mum or have a look online at some of the excellent websites available (see Useful Books and Websites at the end of this book), and do not involve your child.

PICK YOUR FIGHTS

Some things are worth putting your foot down over, while others really are not. If your toddler decides she simply must wear that mismatching hat with an otherwise gorgeous outfit you have put together, go with it — it really doesn't matter that much. Letting her have her own way on the little things will give you ammunition to fight the bigger battles. If you are constantly saying 'no', you'll both get fed-up and your child won't respect your authority as much. Weigh-up the short-term versus the long-term: sometimes, when you're in a rush, for example, you need an easy life in the 'here and now', and you can let some things go; other situations require you to stick to your guns so your child realises it's important, and you will have a smoother ride in the future.

POSITIVE REINFORCEMENT

It should really go without saying that all children need a huge amount of praise and encouragement: in fact, all adults do too. I have found that people generally respond much better to carrots than sticks, I know I do! Your child wants to please you and win your approval. Recognise her achievements and commend them: beam, enthuse, applaud, and then suggest a way of developing what she has already done, reinforcing that it is worthy of time and attention. For instance, if your child presents you with a picture she has just drawn, ask her if she wants to put it on her bedroom wall or maybe draw an even bigger one, and then find her a huge and brightly coloured piece of paper. Make sure all this praise is genuine, though: if you commend her all the time — even when you're both fully aware that she doesn't really deserve it — your words won't mean anything, and she'll have no incentive to try hard next time.

GIVE YOURSELF A BREAK

Most mothers I've spoken to seem to feel guilty some of the time — I seem to feel guilty most of the time! Or maybe it's not guilt, but rather a constant nag at the back of my mind making me forever question whether I'm doing enough as a mother.

My daughter can be perfectly content in the back of the car, chatting away to herself or singing, and I know that sometimes letting her be with her own thoughts and daydreams is extremely important. And yet I feel awful if I'm not interacting with her every minute, stimulating her, and finding the perfect balance between educational conversation and having a great laugh. I know, really, that I'm doing a good job and that driving myself crazy won't help; however, knowing it and chilling out are two different matters entirely!

One of the problems for today's parents is the amount of advice now available, much of it conflicting. A few months ago, my daughter was ill and began sleeping in my bed. I had never previously allowed this for more than a night or two before cracking down and reinforcing our normal routine. Recently, though, she seems much more determined to sleep with me and I can't seem to face the few nights of hell that getting her back in her own bed would involve. I have researched various experts' opinions, which range from 'Don't ever do it', to 'Do it if you're both happy', and I really can't see any reason for forcing her back into her usual routine at the moment: she seems happy and secure and sleeps well; it doesn't disturb my own sleep; I don't have a partner who is being forced onto the sofa or a marriage I am trying to preserve. I do worry a bit about how it will pan-out in the future, but I'm sure she won't be sleeping with me forever!

What I'm trying to say above is, don't angst too much. Think or talk things through, read up on the 'problem' and, if it's not harming anyone, know that it's okay to let it go for a while.

KEEP CALM AND CARRY ON

My married friends all say to me that the things that keep them sane are being able to hand over the baby when their partner gets home from work, and also having adult company in the evening and at weekends. As a single parent, you don't have this comfort and important pressure valve. If your little darling is pressing all the right buttons and you're about to blow, walk away. I have never seen any evidence that smacking works, nor shouting: in fact, both these techniques seem to make children only more frustrated and, in turn, aggressive to others. Quiet but firm communication is the only way: the minute you raise your voice or your hand, your child knows she has won — Game Over.

A TRUTH

Once upon a time, there was a Big Fat Lie. The Lie said, 'you can have it all, Mother'. Mother replied, 'that's not true, you are a Big Fat Lie', and she lived happily ever after.

It is simply not possible for one person to raise a child, work full-time, get enough sleep, and have a social life and some 'me' time; something has to give and you should try to never let it be the time and attention you give to your child. If you have a particularly busy period at work, accept that you may not see your friends much, if at all, during this time. Arranging too much and spreading yourself too thinly will leave you stressed and exhausted. Good parenting demands sacrifices, and only with the sacrifices come the enormous rewards; while a celebrity mother might be able to afford nannies round the clock, just think what she's missing! Accept the restrictions with joy and gratitude: although sleepless nights, nappies and tantrums can feel interminable, each stage of a child's life is relatively short, so enjoy her childhood as much as you possibly can — it'll be over in a flash!

WHAT WORKS?

There is no one right method of parenting, and there are as many variations as there are parents. Ultimately, you must find what works for you and your family and go with it. Your confidence and contentment will shine through and envelop your child with security and warmth.

A MAGIC CALLED LOVE

There's a magic inside all

of us and it's called Love.

Some call it divine…

it certainly works wonders.

MAKING SENSE OF IT ALL

THE ONE

Years ago, as a 'resting' actress, I sold wedding dresses in a Bridal Boutique. I was pretty good at it, making each bride-to-be feel special and taking a genuine interest in her 'how we met' story. But I wanted something in return from this emotionally and often physically naked woman in my charge. 'So, you're sure he's the "one?"', I would ask casually, passing it off as sales girl gossip but scrutinising this lady in love. 'Mmm-hmm' they would confirm, distracted by a neckline or hem, a sleeve or bow. They were always 100% positive that they had found Mr Right, and I wondered whether I would ever be so sure.

A few years later, I was sure and ran myself ragged finding the perfect shoe for the perfect dress and agonising over the colour, the heel, the lace and the words. I had the perfect day with the perfect man — or so I thought. But less than 2 years later, as I carried our first child, my perfect man decided I was not the perfect woman, and left. As I started to recover from the shock and pain, and grew accustomed to the label 'lone parent', I wondered how many of my ex-customers had faced such humiliation and devastation. How many of those 100% sure women had been so utterly sure — as had I — that they had actually gone on to conceive a child with their perfect husband?

I also wondered how a 30-something, worldly-wise, intelligent woman could make such a clang-dinger of a mistake. I have made some pretty colossal screw ups in my time, but I really surpassed myself with this 'one'!

WORKING IT OUT

There are days when just getting through is an achievement. When you're running to stand still and you fall into bed at night, just glad it's all over. But, there are other days when you've had a decent night's sleep, when your little one is being fairly amenable, and your head is a little clearer — and it is these days that can actually be the emotionally toughest because you have the time and energy to ask yourself 'why?', 'how?' and 'what the f*@k?!'

Things went so badly wrong so quickly in my marriage that I hardly saw it coming. Although my husband tells me that he had been trying to talk for months, we had only just married and I was carrying our first child, and I didn't imagine for a moment that the end of our relationship was so close. Being heavily pregnant and then having a newborn baby forced me to get on with everyday

HOW TO BE A HAPPY SINGLE MOTHER   51

life — even though I felt like hiding or running or screaming (and usually all three). For months, I didn't really have the head-space to start questioning why and for what reasons everything had fallen apart and, when I did, it was a very painful process.

It became clear to me that my husband and I are highly incompatible and should probably never have married. But then our amazing daughter would probably not have been born, and that thought convinces me that however much pain, fear and humiliation I had to go through, it was all meant to be: I was meant to get through it all and come out the other side, happier, wiser, stronger — and a mother. I believe that there was no way it could have happened but in the way it did: if my husband had said, "look, I don't love you enough to be with you but I do think we should have a child together", I would never have believed it could work; I didn't want to be a single mum — I wasn't brave enough to take that step.

Whatever your personal circumstances, finding yourself alone can be bewildering, frightening, exhausting and far from the way we hope and dream things will work out. Figuring out what has happened and why is crucial if you are to heal emotionally, but don't force it. Think and talk things over with friends, your ex, or even a professional if you wish, but certainly don't bury your head or rush. Time and a lessening of pain brings clarity and perspective, and truths can present themselves suddenly and unexpectedly.

FACING YOUR OWN MISTAKES

If you were the one who was dumped, it is very easy to apportion all the blame to your ex. If he has been unfaithful, violent, left when you were pregnant or ill, or behaved badly in any way, it is natural for you and your loved ones to blame him for all the problems and the eventual break-up. It may, indeed, be the case that one partner is more 'at fault' than the other, but you must face the part you played. Assuming the role of the victim is often valid and therapeutic initially: you have an obvious target for your anger and can comfort yourself in the knowledge that you were not the one who caused all this misery, which certainly helps when the pain is at its most raw. As your life shifts, however, don't continue to rely on blaming your ex for the fact that you are now alone: dig deep and try to face the mistakes you made. This is not about forgiving someone for treating you badly, although that will, in time, hopefully be achieved; at this point, you are merely trying to recognise that you were an equal, independent person in your marriage/ relationship.

The victim label can be a tough one to shake — especially in the eyes of those who love and care for you — but shake it you must if you are to respect yourself again, realise that you have control and influence over your life, and avoid making the same mistakes again.

ACCEPTANCE

There seem to be a lot of things to accept in a single mother's life. I have come to accept that my ex and I are highly incompatible in many ways, and simply can't be together. I have also had to accept that we may never see eye-to-eye on exactly what went wrong, the reasons why and whose fault it was. But I have also come to realise that it probably doesn't really matter.

> Q. Who will suffer if you bear grudges, hold onto pain and resentment, and live with all that anger?
>
> A. You and your child.
>
> Q. Who will benefit if you accept what has happened and let it go?
>
> A. Everyone.

KEEPING THINGS IN PERSPECTIVE

'What's in a name? That which we call a rose
By any other name would smell as sweet.'
Romeo and Juliet (II, ii, 1-2)

I have agonised for months about my surname. I changed it when I married and considered changing it back when I separated, but I want my daughter and I to have the same name and don't want to change hers. It still does not sit easy sometimes but I have decided to let it be.

Symbolic and poignant things like names and photos can often take on a greater significance than they should. Try to see them for what they are: part of your past which has made you into who you are today. I have had my wedding and engagement rings altered to fit my right hand and wear them as a beautiful piece of modern jewellery. Although my marriage did not work out, it brought me my child and the greatest happiness I have ever experienced. I will not regret or throw out everything to do with my marriage; instead, I am considering putting up some photos of me in my wedding dress, as some of them are wonderful pieces of art, but I'm not ready yet...

NO REGRETS

Don't live your life regretting the choices you've made. If you had never met and committed to your husband/partner, you wouldn't have your child and that — as I hope you'll agree — is not a life worth contemplating.

TURN LEFT FOR HAPPINESS

Most of us seem to grow up with an idea of what we want and what will make us happy. I doubt that being a single mother is anyone's main goal, and does not conjure images of happiness and stability. But, if you find yourself in this situation, you will most likely have to do some pretty hasty re-programming of that life-plan Sat. Nav.; there is no one route guaranteed for happiness.

When something is thrown at us, the person who is most adaptable and flexible is the one who will find the good in adversity, seek out the positive, and turn an apparent disaster into their dream.

MOVING ON

WHAT I'VE LEARNT

You can only toughen-up on your own,
You can only open-up with someone else.

MAKING THE MOST OF BEING SINGLE

HEAD-SPACE AND PEACE:

It's very important not to jump straight from one relationship into another without giving yourself the time and space to heal and re-gather. I have found being single again to be wonderfully liberating; I have rediscovered the joy of my own company and found an inner peace and serenity I have never experienced before. This unexpected calm and contentment gives me such energy and clarity with which to mother my daughter. I am not constantly consumed with anger or confusion; I am not preoccupied with tensions and squabbles; and I am not exhausted by the rollercoaster of emotions always present in a rocky relationship. It has also given me the time to reflect and process what has happened.

I have realised that I cannot rely on anyone else to shoulder my pain and take on the burden of my crap; I must find the strength and courage within me to face my new situation and embrace it fully.

BITE THE BULLET:

It is natural and healthy that two people in a relationship should fall into shouldering the tasks and responsibilities that sit most comfortably with each of them. In every good partnership — whether a personal one or on a business level — each person should play to their own strengths and complement the other.

When you first live on your own there will be jobs that your partner did that you really don't want to do or simply don't know how to do. I loathe spiders and have to force myself to take one outside, but I take a deep breath and go for it; this is the only way I will face this irrational fear, which I really don't want to pass on to my daughter. If you don't know how to check the oil and water in the car, learn; if you hate taking the rubbish out, find a routine which makes it less tedious, like taking it when you're on your way out anyway. See the tasks your partner used to do as just that — tasks. They are not a big deal and they are not emotional pain. Just do them and you'll feel great — you've been through worse, after all!

A NEW RELATIONSHIP

So here you are: back in a place where you didn't think — or hoped — you'd never be in again. Dating as a single parent is a very different game from the heady days before kids. It can be extremely difficult to find time, energy and a place to spend private adult time with a new person. You certainly won't be able to stay up all night chatting or doing anything else! You'll be restricted in many ways, but this doesn't have to mean avoiding new relationships altogether. Below are a few pointers which may ease the way.

SAFETY FIRST:

Never ever put yourself in a situation that may endanger you or your child in any way. Whatever you did pre-motherhood, the rules are different now: you have someone on this earth whose very existence and emotional wellbeing depends on you being fit and well. If you are meeting a new man, do so in a public place, like a restaurant, and make sure a friend knows where you are going. Arrange for her to call you at some point during the evening, and let her know you are okay when you get home. If this new guy takes offence, he's not worth bothering with.

KIDS COME FIRST:

Initially, of course, your dates must be private and conducted in your own time. Keep these times very separate from the rest of your life and keep them away from your home: this is for you alone and should not involve your child at all. Get a babysitter you trust and with whom your child is happy, leave your house, and just enjoy and bit of time and space away from your responsibilities. If, however, your child is ill or properly miserable (not just playing the guilt-trip on you), cancel the date, however late in the day this happens; while it might be extremely disappointing, you won't relax if your child is not happy, and her needs must be put before your own here. You must warn your date in advance that, if a problem arises, you may need to cancel and, again, if he's a decent bloke, he will understand and totally respect your priorities.

PROTECT YOURSELF — PHYSICALLY:

A study into Sexually Transmitted Diseases published last year (*International Journal of Epidemiology*, 14th Nov. 2008) found that far less 30 and 40 year olds use condoms with a new partner than teenagers. If you were in a long-term relationship and took the pill for many years, condoms can take a little getting used to again. Men can often assume that you have sorted out the contraception and, if you don't have a stash of condoms at the ready, they won't either, so be prepared! STDs are blind to age and circumstances, and you don't know who else your new partner may be sleeping with. While you might have been less careful in your pre-baby days, remember your child now and realise it's just not worth the risk.

PROTECT YOURSELF — EMOTIONALLY:

A new man taking an interest in you, complimenting you and making you feel desired and desirable again can be exhilarating and empowering. Your confidence will soar and you'll walk around with a 'cat that got the cream' glow. Enjoy, enjoy! But also look out for yourself.

I don't mean to put a downer on that lovely warm feeling you have, but just go easy. Keep your feet on the ground and really get to know this guy before you get carried away. Someone showing you a little kindness can open the floodgates, and it can be very tempting to start to rely heavily on him for emotional support and fulfilment. But don't give away all that wonderful newfound strength and independence, and don't leave yourself vulnerable and exposed to more heartache by rushing into things and risking the relationship.

Intense feelings can also open up a lot of old wounds. You might think you've healed and moved on, but you'll undoubtedly find that you have a lot more 'baggage' than you think, although this is actually a horribly negative term — I prefer to say 'life experience'. A man of a similar age to you will most probably have past pain and issues he also needs to deal with, but all of this can make you both stronger and more resilient, and can be turned to your advantage in a new relationship.

Remember, too, that a new relationship doesn't have to be full-on if you don't want it to be: your heart is probably a little battered from its last round in the ring. It can also be exhausting and highly frustrating trying to find both opportunity and energy for a relationship that doesn't fit in with the rest of your life and has to be conducted 'after hours'. It may suit you better to build up a friendship with someone first and see where things lead.

Different relationships can fulfil different needs: perhaps one guy is a lovely dinner and theatre companion and you don't want any physical involvement with him. Be true to yourself and open with your date. If you are honest with him and communicate well, you can avoid sending out mixed messages and causing misunderstandings. Never feel pressured to do anything that does not make you entirely comfortable, either physically or emotionally.

AVOIDING THE SAME MISTAKES:

This is where your period of being single should really set you up well. If you rush from one relationship into another, it is easy to repeat mistakes you've made before and fall into the bad habits you had with your ex. Communication is the absolute key: TALK, TALK, TALK. You will both need to be flexible, understanding, patient and supportive, especially if he is a single parent too. Remember the problems you encountered in your past relationship and try to avoid them this time.

INTRODUCING THE KIDS:

Only you can judge when it is the right time to introduce your children to a new partner. I certainly think he should initially be introduced as a platonic friend. You don't need to be all over each other in front of your children anyway, and he needn't be any different from a girl friend popping round. If this relationship does break up, it's going to affect your children a lot less if he's only been around casually and not as a major part of their lives. If you think this new guy may not be Mr Right but only Mr Right Now, don't introduce your kids at all; instead, enjoy spending time with him in your private, adult time, however limited this may be.

ME AGAIN

An inner peace grows in me.
A piece of me that has been missing begins to breathe.

I am Me again.
I am free again.
Free to look and learn and love.

I like this Me,
This peaceful Me.
I smile, I breathe… I live (out breath).

Orit Sutton

Choosing Happiness

We cannot decide what life throws at us, but we can decide how we deal with it. A positive attitude can make the difference between being a miserable victim and a happy, calm person with financial stability, health and love. I once read that you should always imagine you are holding a beautiful and fragrant bouquet, and this idea really makes me smile and feel good. Below I have outlined some more suggestions.

Make Your Home Your Haven

Your child's home should be their rock, their security. One of the huge advantages of being a single parent is that you have complete control over what happens in your own home. Rows and tension create an extremely damaging environment for a child in which to grow up, and now you can ensure that your home is a loving, peaceful and joyous place to be. Fill it with laughter, comfort and stimulation and you and your child will have a safe and happy place to share with others or for quiet times on your own.

If you are working and raising a child alone, finding the time and energy to look after your home can often feel impossible, but see it as an extension of looking after your child: just as you care about her physical health, creating a wonderful space in which your child sleeps, eats and plays is vital for her mental health. I am not suggesting that you employ an interior designer and live in a show flat — rather that you should take pride in your space with some simple techniques, such as:

- Keep on top of clutter so that rooms are as spacious and inviting as possible.
- Make your home a living, breathing space, and don't allow it to stagnate: put up recent paintings your child has done and store old ones, display fresh flowers (even a tiny cheap arrangement) and throw out dead ones, regularly change the toys out on display.
- Have a clearing up time before the dinner/bath/bed routine: involve your child in this by making it a game and give her the responsibility of a couple of toys and books.
- Make the effort to clear away really properly once your child is in bed so that your evening feels adult and ordered.

If your home is a beautiful, happy place, your child will be proud to invite friends over and she will also be more inclined to help you look after it. This calm and attractive space will also be a place for you to think and recharge or to invite your own friends over once your child is settled for the night.

SMILE, SMILE, SMILE!

It is impossible to feel utterly miserable when you smile. Endorphins or 'Happy Hormones' are released into the body when you smile or laugh, and they instantly make you feel better. It may sound rather syrupy, but I make it my rule to smile as I go to sleep and again as I wake in the morning — and it really works.

When things are tough, smiling is often the last thing you feel like doing, but make it a habit and it will soon become natural and spontaneous. Once the smile has made you feel a little happier, you'll want to smile some more, and so the upward, positive spiral progresses! Smiling also attracts people to you, makes you seem more successful, and boosts your immune system… well, it certainly can't hurt!

CELEBRATE YOUR ACHIEVEMENTS

I am terribly bad at this one. When my baby was very young I was delighted when I just managed to get dressed, leave the house by midday and then cook some dinner. Now I'm not satisfied unless I've earned some cash, taught my daughter a vital life skill, ticked off 49 jobs from my 'To Do' list, and achieved it all with immaculate hair and nails. I am often so preoccupied with what I haven't managed to get done or what I have to do the next day, that I often forget to take a few moments to enjoy my successes.

The relentless and often exhausting job of mothering doesn't always have obvious accomplishments, but if you've given your child lots of love and attention, you've achieved a huge amount right there. It's great to have high standards, but unrealistic aims can leave you feeling extremely frustrated and are counter productive.

If necessary, spend a few moments before you go to bed writing down what you have achieved that day. Remember to include seemingly small things, like having cooked a healthy meal or having had a good walk with your child.

CHANGE YOUR PERSPECTIVE

On the flip side, try not to see mistakes and difficult times as failures. Instead, view them as experiences that have made you who you are and from which you can learn.

SURROUND YOURSELF WITH HAPPY, LOVING PEOPLE

When I decided to go it alone with my daughter, I vowed that I would surround the two of us with wonderful people — and I have done. Positive, happy people are infectious and will lift your mood; negative people, on the other hand, will drain your energy and your spirits. Acknowledge that you and your child deserve to be happy and you will automatically prevent anyone who endangers that happiness to be in your lives. With this attitude, you will find that the negative people start to drop away, and more and more positive ones will surround you.

As a single parent, you will need a support network which can help you physically, mentally and emotionally. Be a super friend and relative; remember everyone's birthdays and stay in touch, especially when someone is having a hard time or has something to celebrate (a quick email will do and only takes a couple of minutes). It feels good to make others feel loved and remembered, and it will also create a pool of people who love you and want to be there for you.

Your child also needs regular contact with family members and friends, and you cannot possibly supply all the attention and stimulation she needs all of the time; different people can provide variety and a connection with the outside world.

PHYSICAL CONTACT

Just as you need to nurture your heart and spirit, your body also needs care and attention. Physical contact need not be sexual: I have a girlfriend who made sure she booked in for regular massages when she first split up with her husband. The feeling of being touched by another human is vital for your general well-being so, as well as your child, cuddle your friends and hold hands with your sister!

BE INSPIRED!

Read about people/women/single mums who have done incredible stuff. Talk to people who live their dreams. Positive successful people will stimulate, challenge and boost your confidence and will light your way...

BE GOOD TO YOURSELF

◆   Spend a few minutes on yourself everyday and you'll feel a lot better. Pluck your eyebrows, wash your hair regularly and keep your nails in good condition. You can do all this at home and not spend a penny on it! If you let yourself become a mess, you'll feel much less like getting out there and getting on with life. Never, ever just pop to the shops wearing a stained top and not a scrap of make-up — you never know who you might meet; a potential business partner, perhaps; the headmistress of that school you really want to get your child into; or maybe the love of your life...

◆   Try to do some regular exercise. This will not only make you look and feel better in the short-term, but will also give you a better chance of seeing your child grow up! You don't need to join an expensive gym and put yourself through hell — just try to walk, cycle or go swimming with your child; she'll be getting some exercise too and you'll spend some lovely time together.

◆ Feed yourself healthy nourishing food as if you are feeding your child, and really consider what you put inside your body.

◆ Make sure that you have a little time for yourself. If you are lucky enough to be fulfilled by your job, this might be enough. If not, try to have a hobby that is just for you and for pure enjoyment.

◆ Once a week, get a babysitter, glam yourself up, and go out — your child will be fine and you certainly deserve it!

SING AND DANCE

Just like exercise, singing and dancing releases endorphins and forces you to take in more oxygen. On a rainy day, whack on some loud music and bop about with your child: you'll both feel great!

THE GRASS IS NOT ALWAYS GREENER

Even the most perfect-looking family has its problems: that beautiful woman you see on the school-run who has the gorgeous, supportive husband, two clean kids and a big house will certainly have difficult areas in her life — everyone does. Perhaps her parents live miles away and the children rarely see their grandparents; maybe she has a health problem. I'm certainly not suggesting we wish others ill, but don't be fooled by appearances, or allow yourself to fall into the trap of envying someone else's life.

Everything is relative. If you meet or read about someone who really has a hell of a lot on their plate, it can clarify the great things in your own life. There is nothing more humbling than watching the news and witnessing parents who have no food, water or medicine for their children; it certainly gives me a sharp reminder of just how lucky I really am, if I ever need one.

COUNT YOUR BLESSINGS — LITERALLY

Think about or write down all the good things in your life. There will be the obvious ones but you'll also discover ones that you hadn't even registered before. Acknowledging even the smallest of blessings will give them weight, and they will become things to really celebrate.

HAVE A HAPPY TRIGGER

Create a happy trigger that can quickly remind you of a person or time with happy associations. Many people carry a photo of their child for just this purpose: a quick glance can instantly relieve stress and lift your spirits. I have set all my passwords on my email accounts, online banking and other logins to a positive phrase or inspiring word, and whenever I login to an account, my word or phrase acts as a positive mantra.

CONTROL YOUR THOUGHTS

Your thoughts are just thoughts. It may feel as if they pop into your head and you have no control over them, but this is not the case: you are in control of what you think, how you react to situations, the way people and circumstances make you feel and, ultimately, how happy you are. It will take time and practice, but you can control what you think and feel.

Try to turn difficult situations on their heads and see them from a different angle. Instead of viewing the break-up of your marriage as a tragedy, for example, try acknowledging the freedom and inner peace that being single can bring. You are now a stronger person — not a victim — with exciting opportunities ahead of you should you wish to embrace them.

When a negative or difficult thought enters your head don't allow it the luxury of settling in and making itself comfy. Acknowledge it, see it for what it is — just a thought — and replace it with another more pleasant/exciting/happy thought. You can pick anything, but it has to be big enough to do the job. Think of your child, a friend that makes you feel good or a recent achievement you've made, even if it's a small one like sorting out that chaotic cupboard! At first, you'll have to consciously work at replacing negative thoughts with positive ones, but it'll soon become a habit and the negative ones will eventually drop away altogether.

HAVE A CONFIDANTE

It's probably not a great idea to tell or show everything you are feeling and thinking to everyone. However, talking and working through what has happened is vital if you are to heal emotionally and be able to move on. Some people around you will be more able to cope with this process than others.

When I first found myself alone, I was too shocked and devastated to consider who I talked to. I would cry and verbally 'vomit' on anyone who came anywhere near me. But after a while, I was able to be a little less selfish (although my loved ones would not consider I had been), and be more selective. There are some people who are fantastic listeners and incredibly supportive, and they took the brunt of my emotional outbursts. But it's these very people, of course, who love and care about me the most and therefore worry about me the most. Sometimes, if there is someone else around who can lend an ear and a shoulder, I will try not to worry my nearest and dearest. If I want to let off some steam, shout, cry and swear rather I lot, I now try to choose someone who won't worry themselves sick all night, and it also saves me from having to worry about them!

BE SPONTANEOUS

Every now and then, forget all the organising and planning (see Getting It All Done), scoop up your child and have fun: let her walk on walls, skip down the street together, have a rough and tumble on the grass, paint her face, eat cakes…

OTHER PEOPLE

I was in the chemist with my daughter recently when she spotted something familiar on the shelf behind the checkout assistant. "Daddy has that", she said pointing. "Does he?" I replied. "Did you see it at Daddy's house?" The checkout assistant's head jerked up before she had time to hide her shock and curiosity. I carried on chatting to my daughter, deliberately allowing the assistant to hear our conversation: what did she expect me, a single parent, to look like? A monster with three heads, monosyllabically grunting at my child as she stuffed chips into her malnourished mouth? As we left the chemist I hoped that this ignorant woman had seen a rather more positive image of a single-parent family, and I refused to let her behaviour affect my good mood: we can't control everything that happens to us but we can control how we react to it.

BE PROUD

Walk tall, hold your head up high, feel good in your own skin, celebrate your uniqueness, love your shape, like who you are and recognise what you have to offer… try one or two of these well known feel-good techniques: they really do work!

IT'S YOUR LIFE

It's your life, so it's up to you to decide how you want to spend it - now. It is totally within your power to live a happy and secure life. If your child grows up with a confident, positive and inspiring mother, she will have the best possible example of how to live a happy life herself. Love yourself and your life and you will have more love and energy for your child — everyone wins!

YOUR 3-STEP ACTION PLAN TO HAPPINESS

1. Decide you want to be happy

2. Acknowledge that your happiness is in your own hands

3. Make it happen

Attitude is more important than facts. It is more important than the past, than education, than money, than circumstances, than failures, than success, than what other people think or say or do. It is more important than appearance, giftedness or skill. It will make or break a company, a home, a relationship. The remarkable thing is we have a choice, every day regarding the attitude we will embrace for the day. We cannot change our past. We cannot change the fact that other people will act in a certain way. We cannot change the inevitable. The only thing we can do is play on the one string we have, and that is our attitude. I am convinced that life is 10% what happens to me and 90% how I react to it.

Charles Swindoll

LIFE

I only have one and it's mine,
To do with as I please.
I shall not fit in a box, wear a label or fulfil a target.
Criticise, stifle, judge or neglect me and I shall turn from you
and run to the light,
Breathless and gleeful with anticipation of the new.
Support, love and understand me and I shall be there for you
tenfold.
I have a clear mind, open heart and free spirit,
And I cherish these days: each and every one.

Orit Sutton

HOPES AND DREAMS

KEEP THEM ALIVE!

The person you were pre-marriage, pre-motherhood, pre-separation and pre-divorce need not be lost. What did you dream about? What got you up in the morning? You may not have the time, freedom or energy to actively pursue your wildest ambitions right now, but there will be a time when you can resurrect them. Keep them safe, write them down, and even start to live them. Visualising the life you want can work miracles and open doors in the most unexpected ways and places.

Be open and receptive to the fact that your dreams and goals may have actually changed. Motherhood puts things into perspective and teaches us what's really important: although we all want financial security, perhaps wealth is no longer so important to you; travelling the world may have pre-occupied your younger days but a happy home with your child may be far more attractive now, and there is always time to travel and explore later in life. Maybe you are actually living your dream right now — you just have to recognise it!

IN CONCLUSION

What I have set out in this book are ideals. It's great to have high standards but there is also the need to be realistic. I aim to do much of what I have written here for you, but never manage to achieve it all. Set your goals, work hard to achieve them and succeed. And then, sometimes say, 'sod it all!' Let your child stay up late during a holiday and eat take-away pizza in front of the tele, leave her with her dad or grandma and go out, party, let your hair down.

None of what I have suggested is easy, emotion-free or ever complete. It is a work in progress, a journey, an exploration. Make mistakes, cry and scream (when your child is not around), chat to your friends and family and professionals if it helps, and then pick yourself up and carry on.

I don't have all the answers — far from it. I am constantly learning and forging forwards and falling back, and some memories still drive fear and panic through my gut. But, this is not peculiar to single mums — it's called Life and I love this wild, challenging, overwhelming, amazing ride!

Come with me. Don't be a victim. Don't excuse your failings because you're a lowly single mother. Let's show 'em what we're made of... come on, let's go!

FOR MY GIRL

*Within me you were realised and I gave you my blood and
nourishment and energy.*
And when you emerged and the cord was severed,
*You suckled from my breast, greedy and impatient, sucking the
very fat from my bones.*
Dearest daughter, in my heart and soul that cord still binds us.
*When you turn to me I feel it yank and reel you into my
embrace:*
*When you run wild and glorious I lengthen it and allow your
spirit to fly free.*
*I do not own you but I am blessed to guide you, protect you,
nurture and love you.*
Thank you.

Mummy

USEFUL BOOKS AND WEBSITES

USEFUL BOOKS

'The Complete Single Mother' by Andrea Engber and Leah Klungness, Ph.D.

'Toddler Taming' by Dr. Christopher Green

USEFUL WEBSITES

Specialists in part-time work and flexible employment:

www.womenlikeus.org.uk

www.jobs4mothers.com

www.workingmums.co.uk

National Childminding Association:

www.ncma.org.uk

Single Parenting:

www.oneparentfamilies.org.uk

www.gingerbread.org.uk

Home-Start, supporting parents who are finding it hard to cope:
www.home-start.org.uk
Sure Start, giving kids the best start in life:
www.surestart.gov.uk

Parentscentre, helping you to help your child:
www.parentscentre.gov.uk

Helplines for confidential emotional support:
www.samaritans.org
www.befrienders.org

CONTACT ME

If you have found this book useful or have any suggestions, or if you'd like to share your own experiences with me or need a little advice, please do drop me a line: I'd love to hear from you!

My email address is: orit.singlemother@live.com

Lightning Source UK Ltd.
Milton Keynes UK
UKOW050000240413

209655UK00014B/708/P